My Paranormal Journey

A quick look back at how I got started.

By Author

Wayla Duley

Preface

As a child Wayla Duley was always interested in the unknown. Late night horror films and visiting haunted places was a common occurrence. Wayla was captivated with finding out the truth.

The author was born into a Christian family who believed in the Supernatural and most of the family members also believe in the Paranormal.

My Paranormal Journey was written not only to give firsthand accounts into the paranormal, but also with the hope that others might not feel so afraid when something unexplained happens to them.

Many people experience paranormal events and never report them because they are afraid what people might think. They are not alone and perhaps will benefit from reading the short version of Wayla Daley's own paranormal journey.

Acknowledgements

I give the highest honor and respect to God whose name is <u>**Jehovah**</u>. Thank you for waking me up every day and for believing in me. Without you nothing is possible.

Exodus 3:13-15

Then Moses said to God, "If I come to the people of Israel and say to them, 'The God of your fathers has sent me to you,' and they ask me, 'What is his name?' what shall I say to them?" God said to Moses, "I am who I am." And he said, "Say this to the people of Israel, 'I am has sent me to you.'"

God also said to Moses, "Say this to the people of Israel, 'The Lord, the God of your fathers, the God of Abraham, the God of Isaac, and the God of Jacob, has sent me to you.' This is my name forever, and thus I am to be remembered throughout all generations.

Psalms 83:18

That men may know that thou, whose name alone is **JEHOVAH**, art the most high over all the earth.

Mathew 6:9-13

Our Father, which art in heaven, Hallowed be thy Name. Thy Kingdom come. Thy will be done in earth, as it is in heaven. Give us this day our daily bread. And forgive us our trespasses, as we forgive them that trespass against us. And lead us not into temptation, but deliver us from evil. For thine is the kingdom, the power, and the glory, For ever and ever. Amen.

Introduction

Today, I have decided to start this journal. I don't want to forget anything that has happened in my life. I also in part write this journal because I'm not sure how to make sense of some of the things that has happened because they are so incredible.

My experiences with the paranormal have answered many questions that I had growing up. Some have left me with more questions that remain unanswered. Maybe through the course of this book and the subsequent others we can figure out the answers together.

As you continue to read through this book you will find many things that will be hard for you to understand or for that matter believe. I will do my best to explain and detail each event. Who knows, you may even read something that will scare you. Don't be alarmed I will teach you how to protect yourself.

If you so choose to continue on, grab a buddy and cuddle up under the covers. Make sure to tuck in all sides, lest something crawl under there with you.

If you do become afraid as you are reading, just be glad it was me it happened to. One thing is for sure, you won't look at things the same way again. So without further ado let's begin here.

Interview with KAV

The event took place a couple of years ago when I was 10 or 11 years old. I was at home in the living room watching TV as my mom lay in bed sick.

Our house was built many years ago and the original owners had died. My grandfather died in the house several years later or about a couple of years before this happened.

I am almost sure that an Indian was buried nearby sometime in the past.

I believe that growing up with a mom who has an open mind has made me more able to experience things. I sometimes hear talking that no one else hears, and I sometimes see things no one else sees at the time.

While my mom was sick in bed, and I knew that I was the only other person in the house because my dad was at work, I looked over at her room. I could see her from where I was sitting lying on her bed, and I saw a black figure move past her door in her room.

It completely blocked my view of her for a split second. I went into her room and woke her up after I checked the closets and under the bed making sure no one was in there.

I asked her who was in there with her. She hadn't even noticed it. I believe in GOD and I believe in the paranormal. Nothing unusual was going on recently, other than my mom was sick.

I have had several other experiences in that house and in other places as well. I don't think I'm crazy at all. I saw it with my two own eyes and still have a perfectly good memory of it.

I may be young but I know what I saw and I have seen these shadow people on more than one occasion. I am not afraid of them even though I think they are demons.

I believe that people are given gifts from God and we ought to learn how to use them and not be so closed minded and call these gifts demonic or of the devil.

Chapter One

The first thing I should tell you is that my name is Wayla. My husband's name is Hector and our sons name is Kristian. We have four dogs. An Alaskan Husky/Border collie mix, a Chocolate Labrador Retriever, and two German Shepherds puppies named Lilly and Dora. Lilly and Dora are investigators, ghost hunters, in training. We also have a cat and a duck as well.

I was born in the boot heal of Missouri in the early 1970's and lived most of my life in central Michigan. I have traveled the world to many countries but decided to settle in Southeast Louisiana.

I am an ordained minister and have several years of college, but I prefer to do physical labor as it makes me feel good to work with my hands.

My husband is from Ahuachapán, El Salvador. He once refused to completely believe in things that defy explanation despite his own experiences.

My son has never done anything but believe. He honestly never had a choice in the matter. I raised him with an open mind as best as I could just like my father tried with me. Maybe it's better that way. Kristian has no fear of the unknown or the unexplained.

I always believed the paranormal might have an affect on him in such a way as to make him afraid of even his own shadow. To my surprise it is all normal to him and has not had a frightful effect on him. I see him becoming a strong person with his head firmly on his shoulders.

You can claim it was my imagination all you want if it makes you feel less afraid. But I would like for you to answer me just one of these questions:

When an infant, who does not walk or talk yet and has had no life experiences to date, looks around the room seemingly following something invisible or laughs at the ceiling what do you suppose has the child's attention?

Better yet, does your child have an imaginary friend?

Maybe your child is afraid to sleep alone claiming someone is in their room?

Does your child hate a location with a passion or refuse to go into a room or a place without reason?

While you ponder these questions and think back about all the times you have had at least one of these happen to you or someone you know let me now tell you how to protect yourself with a cleansing white light that will hold you and protect you whenever you feel fearful or feel the need for comfort.

The best thing is to do is to pray, but for those who do not believe in prayer or God try following the instructions on the next page.

Calling the white light

Sit in a comfortable seat. Relax in peace and quiet for a few minutes. Clear your mind of all stresses. Now imagine a warm and bright white light starting to form at your belly just about 6 inches from your body.

See how beautiful and comforting this light truly is. You can feel the tingle on your skin as the light grows brighter.

See the comforting white light begin to spread over your body enveloping you from head to toe without leaving one spot uncovered.

Continue to sit there watching the protective light shimmer all around you and feel the warmth and peace coming from the light. Feel the safety within the light.

You are now protected from fear. Relax and hold on to this comforting light for as long as you need to. When you are ready, begin reading.

Anytime you should begin to feel fearful call on the white light. It is there and is protecting you. It is comforting you and warming you. Just relax and recall the light to protect and calm you.

Something About Ghost Hunting.

A Poem by Kristian V.

I hear a BOO!

I need a clue,

What's that BOO!

I get a touch,

Like a bunch.

There's an Electromagnetic field,

I should have brought my shield.

What's that sound?

It's coming out of the ground,

Over there near that mound,

And from all around.

I hear that BOO!

What do I do?

Oh no, I think I'm through!

LORD, I NEED YOU!

Chapter Two

Let's me share with you a few of my childhood experiences. I believe this is the best way to get this journal started and lay out some background on myself.

One of the very first memories I have is as a child is that of a stuffed wolf with a plastic face. I had been given this toy by my mother as a child.

The face was somewhat grotesque and even as an adult made me very uneasy. It didn't matter where this toy was in my room I couldn't sleep. It, yes the toy, wouldn't let me or so I believed at the time.

When the lights were turned out I would have to cover my head because if I didn't I would see this stuffed wolf move its head and its face would change, morphing into something even more frightening. I was terrified of that wolf.

My name means wolf in one Native American language and graceful one in another. Perhaps that was why she gave me that horrible toy as a kind of token or something you would use as a spirit animal, but it wasn't for me.

I don't believe that spirit guides should scare you. I haven't seen that wolf for many, many years and I plan to keep it that way.

The first event that I can remember, the one that I believe changed my life forever, is a dream. Yes a dream. Sounds silly, but it is true.

I was plagued by this crazy dream over and over again, night after night, again and again. This dream never wavered in content from the original or first night I dreamed it.

I was about 6 years old and quickly becoming very afraid to sleep. It wasn't that creepy wolf toy making me unable to sleep this time, thank God, but this dream was something so much more.

I know, I know, blame it on TV or the movies and that would be a wonderfully acceptable explanation if I hadn't been born to a very dedicated religious family. We didn't go to the movies or watch a lot of TV.

Let's take a little side step here. When I was born my mother was just 7 months pregnant with me. She told me that I didn't want to stay in the womb and she had many problems with the pregnancy.

The end result was that I was born premature at 7 months and weighed only 4 pounds. I was 10 inches long and born not breathing. I was a blue baby.

The doctors worked on me for several (45 to be exact) minutes to get me to breath and when I finally did they informed my father what was going on. Ok back to my story now.

After years of being plagued by this dream something strange started happening to me and within me. I will explain more about that later on if you bear with me.

As I said before I was about six years old. I was living with my Aunt Genevieve and her husband Bill. My parents were in the middle of a very messy divorce that took a small fortune and three and a half years to complete.

One night I went to bed as usual. I wore a pale green baby doll gown. The gown had a chiffon layer over it. That beautiful gown made me feel like a princess. It was my aunts old night gown from the 1960's.

Little did I know that I would wake up the next morning after having dreamed a dream that would change me forever.

My Dream:

I opened my eyes to see a girl in a twin sized bed on the other side of a wooden nightstand that was between us in what seemed to be our beds. The room was huge and very retro with wood panel walls, avocado carpet and dated furniture.

I was confused because I didn't know where I was so I sat up in the bed. When I did, a huge, ghostly, white gloved hand came out of the wall and tried to grab the girl.

I tried to scream but no sound would come out. She woke up at that instant seeing the hand she ran out of the room to some place unknown to me.

Suddenly I was alone and frightened. My uncle Bill came walking in talking, but I couldn't hear a word coming out of his mouth.

All of a sudden a giant man sized brown bear wearing a white t-shirt with a white plastic face mask appeared in the room behind him.

It looked something like that popular kids TV show only brown. My uncle turned around and saw this bear and pulled a rope from his pocket and put the rope around the neck of the bear and they both vanished right before my very eyes.

The girl came back from parts unknown and we decided to go and look for my father. We walked over to the door and knelt down. She pulled the door open very slowly, but just a crack so that we could see what the hallway was like.

We looked out into the hallway and there were robots in the hall walking back and forth. Yes, bright and shiny Killer robots.

We slowly sneaked around avoiding the killer robots and found the room where my father was. As we walked in we noticed that the room was made almost the same as ours with the wood panels on the walls and the same avocado carpet, but it was somewhat more ornate.

My dad was sitting on a round bed. This bed was clothed in red velvet and had steps leading up all around it as if they were tiers on a gilded birthday cake. These tiers were golden in color and had alternating round red and white lights around them like you might imagine a spaceship would have. My dad looked like a king sitting on this bed.

My dad gave us words of encouragement to the tune of ' You will always have each other ' and other things similar. I can't quite remember exactly what he had said but I do remember he was kneeling there in the top of the bed looking down at me and the girl sitting on one of the tiers.

He was wearing a creamy white shirt and an amber colored sweater vest. His smile was so warm and lovely. When all of a sudden the top tier of his bed detached and began to float up towards the ceiling.

He was still giving his words of wisdom when the ceiling opened up and dad just floated away and the ceiling closed back up. The girl and I just sat there for a while crying.

We were sad we got left behind by my father, but we knew we couldn't stay there so we returned to our room. I sat down on my bed and she lay down on hers.

Suddenly that same ghostly hand stretched forth again and this time it was able to take the girl away through the wall leaving me all alone screaming in terror afraid of what was to happen next.

That was my dream in a nut shell. I was plagued by this dream night after night for quite some time. I was so afraid to sleep and dream this dream again that my uncle Bill would stay up all night with me if need be and hold me. I got to where I had to sleep on a cot in his room to protect me from these dreams.

Now you might ask what is so scary about this dream. First of all remember I was not even seven years old yet and I was having this same dream without one detail changing every night. My aunt would put a Bible under my pillow to stop the dreams.

I know what you are thinking, but Elvis was still alive and Star Wars was yet to come out over two years later. I did mention that I came from a very dedicated Christian family and we weren't allowed much TV and certainly no outside 'weirdoes' even in the 1970s were allowed around us.

Anyway, I prayed and begged God for many years to stop these dreams. They scared me and I thought that I was being oppressed by the devil.

I now believe that God had a reason for me to dream them because of what was to come afterwards. Believe me when I tell you that I was not prepared for what was about to begin happening to me.

I soon began to experience Deja Vu and have prophetic dreams about future events that would ultimately come true in their entirety, but that is another chapter in this journal and I will leave it at that for now. No, I am not crazy.

I would continue to grow up and have these dreams again being plagued night after night twice more. Once at almost 14 years of age and again at nearly 21. They still unnerved me and freaked me out.

I begged God again and again to please not let me dream any more. I can only guess that these other two occasions were booster dreams, something like booster shots. Who knows maybe I was actually abducted by aliens and they implanted this dream in me.

Still to this day I get chills thinking about the dream that happened night after night without fail. I also think about how the details in the dream never changed. So very strange to not waver at all, not even one minute detail.

Logic would suppose that some small detail would be different, but it never was, and this is probably the single most terrifying factor in this situation.

Interview with Tammy A.

It was 1994 and I was at home. I believe in God, but I also believe that spiritual things happen. I'm not psychic, but I do, at times, have a kind of knowledge.

One night I felt someone standing in my bedroom door. It felt peaceful. I just knew someone had died, but I wasn't sure who it was. Some days later I found out that my cousin on my dad's side had been murdered.

When he came to me that night in my room he sat down on the side of the bed and kissed my cheek. I said I'm sorry you are gone, but please leave. I feel like he waved goodbye and left.

It was a couple of weeks before I found out who had died. And a couple of weeks before he died I dreamed someone similar to him had died. I couldn't see who it was clearly at the time.

When I found out about my cousin, he had in fact been murdered just exactly like in my dream. I later spoke with his sister and found out that he had sat on her bed too.

Chapter Three

I began to experience Deja Vu, as I mentioned in the previous chapter. This was something so very uncontrollably scary for me. At first it was somewhat of an amusement to my friends.

We would go somewhere and sit down like at the donut shop or fast food place. I would begin say the exact words at the exact same time as the people in the next booth as if I were reading from the same script.

People who knew me would watch me. They would see me turn my back and mouth the words along with the complete strangers as they were saying them.

The more I think about it, the funnier it seems, now. At the time all of this was happening I wasn't keen on the idea, but little did I know that this would grow into a completely different monster.

Quickly, and I do mean quickly, this progressed into dreams. No, not the same dream as I had before, but something even more strange and terrifying to me.

Are you ready for it? My dreams would come true. Why on Earth didn't I know or imagine this was coming after being able to 'know' what people were saying is beyond me, but I had absolutely no clue.

Once again I was afraid to sleep and afraid to dream. With every night I grew that much more afraid. I did not want to know the future. NO, NO, NO not me, not the future.

It started off innocently enough though. I dreamed I was walking home from the neighbor's house that lived across the street one night. An older olive green car was passing me on the street and it slowed down greatly as it passed me. There were two men in dark suits in the car. The men were staring me down as they passed. The very next day it happened. I know it's something normal that could happen in real life.

Then another dream came. I was in the playground of the middle school swinging on the swings with another girl. Two very grown males in long black trench coats approached and spoke to us. I couldn't see their faces because they seemed to be erased in my dream, but I remembered everything else.

A couple days later I was able to see their faces in real life. They were every bit 20-30 years old and they seemed a little strange, almost odd. I was terrified because my dream was coming true.

I struggled to remember what was going to happen next. My stress was on the rise and I was nearly in a fight or flight mode. Two teenage girls alone near the woods behind the school was dangerous situation to be in.

They did not harm us nor did my dream indicate that they would. It was a little hard to get away from them because they followed us when we left. We started to get scared then.

I had begun to keep a dream journal so that I wouldn't forget a single vivid detail. I dropped this practice after a year or so because I was being terrorized by my dreams and more so by the realizations that my dreams were coming true and I couldn't tell anyone because I would be considered crazy or worse possessed by the devil.

"GOD, please, please, please don't let me dream tonight. I beg you GOD please don't let me dream" Was my prayer every night for many years.

I could not sleep until I was so exhausted that I passed out and then I only slept 4 hours a night and sometimes only sleeping 12 hours in the entire week. I still do this today.

Maybe this is extreme to you, but to me this was my life. Even my father couldn't understand it either. My grandmother was somewhat of a physic according to my dad and his sister and even my dad had dreams.

I was so terrorized by these prophetic dreams. I did not want to know what was going to happen or who was going to walk through the door. I didn't want to know the person in the store at the malls personal business or what anyone was going to say. I wanted to be surprised. No, I wanted to be normal.

For years I begged God to stop all together and entirely these abilities. I honestly believed that they were evil. I was also taught that things like these were to be avoided, by our church, unless it was a gift from GOD. I did not know how to tell if it was a gift from God or not. I was too scared to ask someone.

I did not under any circumstances want to go to hell. So I worked very hard at blocking these things in addition to praying.

Finally they slowed down to about one quarter the frequency and something new began to happen. As if these dreams weren't bad enough, I have to be forever changing and developing new abilities for some unknown reason.

Soon I was able to read people. Yes, I was able to 'KNOW' complete strangers. This is something that is hard for me to explain but I need to try so that you might understand what I mean.

I can meet new people and somehow I get this feeling that comes over me. If the person is less than reputable then I feel this pressure in the back of my head and I for some reason cannot stand to be near them. Even becoming rude or slightly hostile (non-violent) towards them. It is not my intention it's my body or mind or something causing this to happen.

The longer I am around the person the more I know about them. I try to issue the benefit of the doubt telling myself that I am wrong about the person. I force myself to attempt to be around these people whom something about me can't stand, but it only stresses me out and makes me sick. A good example of this type of person would be if someone does illegal drugs, is a thief or into bad things or whatever.

I am never wrong about anyone. This has caused me a great deal a grief. It has upset a few people when they asked me why I don't want to be around someone because I told them about that person. They would get mad at me but soon they would find out I was right and ask me how I knew. My only explanation was/is I just get this feeling that they were doing drugs or whatever.

I carry with me the remainder of these abilities to this day and have yet to misread someone or be incorrect in my dreams or the spoken words of complete strangers. I feel like this is somehow changing now. I'm ready for the change this time. I am no longer afraid.

People began to trust me when I would tell them to not go somewhere because something would happen or don't trust that person. Yet it unnerved them a little. I have since cut off most contact with people because it isn't good for me to subject myself to much of this. It makes me uneasy and stressed.

The only person who never freaked out about any of the things that was happening to me and who never told me I was allowing the devil to have access to my soul was my dad when he figured out what I could do.

When I was younger I did some things that were frightening in their own right, because of a lack of knowledge and understanding. I am ashamed of them now, but at the time I was having fun.

I began to familiarize myself with magick. My father taught me some nature magick that his mother taught him and it captivated me. I use the word magick because society today has it labeled as such and believe it something of the devil, which it is not. It is simply abilities or knowledge of things that we no longer possess and have forgotten due to time and lack of use much like an ancient language. This scares some people while others are intrigued and embrace it.

My father told me that there are things in life that we just could not possibly understand and that the old ways, the way of his mother, were quickly being lost.

One example of this would be when my father was bothered by warts on his fingers, chest, knees, and feet etc. His mother taught him how to remove them without medicine. She taught him there are ways of getting things done. And they worked without fail.

Well call some of these things 'old wives tales' or 'holistic remedies' today. A friend was also bothered by warts as well on his fingers. I was not bothered by them until I was nearly thirty years old and still have only had two in my lifetime.

My friend wanted them burned off at the doctor and would not listen to my dad on how to get rid of them. I did though. When I was about 13 years old I had another friend who had a very bad one on her finger and I showed her what to do. We did it together and her wart was gone in a few short days.

Nowadays this kind of healing is also sometimes considered sacred knowledge or magick and even alchemy. I have always been one who refuses narcotics and synthetics if I can. I prefer natural ways of healing.

I have had many doctors get very mad at me and ask me why I even bother to come in if I am not going to take the medicine they prescribed. I would just say I wanted to make sure it wasn't something requiring serious medicine and if he knows of something natural that I could take.

I will always opt for eating something or taking something natural before I will put any type of medicine in my body. I make sure that it comes from a trusted source first.

If you can gather your own ingredients and make your own it is even better that the store bought ones. If you do make your own then **you need to understand what you are doing** and maybe have someone help you who makes these natural medicines the first time or so.

Please always put the best quality and most pure natural remedies in your body. Don't believe hype and advertisement. Research and learn. Be fully informed.

Interview with Hector V.

I was 22 years old I was walking home alone through a coffee plantation in El Salvador. It was around 5pm. It was alright with the owners that I walk through their property. They were nice people. I remember they would give their workers beautiful gifts for Christmas.

I was walking, getting some exercise. I decided to walk through this plantation. It was about two months after harvest and everything was quiet. I was a little tired and decided to sit down and rest for a few moments.

I walked just inside the woods beside the fields where I could sit next to a tree and relax. As I walked into the woods it was as if someone had poured out a lot of coffee fruit onto the ground. I decided to pick as much up as I could. I made a bag from my shirt. Coffee is worth a lot of money in my country.

As I was picking up the coffee that had been spilled out onto the ground I moved leaves to pick up more and more. After moving some of the leaves I saw a new coffee plant growing with two branches on it.

The branches began to twist and formed a Virgin Mary with the baby and Halo. The more coffee I picked up the more was there. Every time I tried to grab the plant it would become limbs again and it would return to the Virgin when I would stop trying to grab it.

I left the coffee and made a mark on a big tree. I left because it was getting dark and I didn't want to be out after dark in our civil war torn country. I was thinking I would come back the next day. When I got home I wanted to tell someone very badly.

My neighbor was 94 years old. His name was Jose. I told him the story and he told me that I should have not told anyone because it was something magical God had for me and that I would never see it again.

The next day I went there alone again and could not find the mark on the tree that I had made nor the plant or the coffee for that matter.

I returned home saddened by this and saw Jose again and I told him I couldn't find anything. He informed me that God and the Virgin had something planed for me and I would never know it now. To this day I have no clue as to what it was nor have I ever seen it again.

If this happened to me it can happen to anyone. I was poor with a great need at the time. I believe in God and in happenings that are unexplainable. I never thought I was crazy. It left me wanting more and to know what it was and why.

I am not interested in whether or not someone believes me. I don't even really like talking about these things after what happened when I told someone.

Chapter Four

When my father was in the process of divorcing my mother he bought a small two bedroom house in the suburbs of Flint, Michigan. This was in 1977.

The brother of the original owners sold it to my dad. He was a short man about 5'5" and maybe 140lb. His age was around 60 yet he still had very dark chestnut colored hair.

I was standing there when my dad asked why he had sold it so cheaply. The man said it was because he was the last of the family and there he had no use for the home so he sold it to my dad.

The man would come around from time to time and talk with my father. People were neighborly back in those days, or did he know something he wasn't saying?

His brother and sister-in-law had died in the house we later found out. They had left a button stand, which I still have, and a cherry wood rocking chair in the house which would later become the source of many a night of terror for me.

At first I was just there on the weekends because my mother had custody of me and my father had visitation rights. I was with him on the weekends and during the summer.

As I alluded to before that house had a very unsettling nature about it. Ten months passed and the courts awarded my father with custody of me.

After I settled in and became more comfortable in the home strange things didn't go unnoticed, nor could I tell myself it was my imagination any longer.

On many occasions I would hear something in the living room and I would get out of bed and creep around to look. It was very dark but you could see the reflection of a balding man in the TV. I suppose that I don't have to tell you that this scared me through and through. I was only 7 or 8 at the time.

You could be sitting reading or watching TV and see a black shadow standing in the corner as if it was waiting for someone or something. This was the first ghost I recall experiencing in the house. I would go on and experience something else though.

Black Shadow People are kind of a strange but common thing. They are considered to be bad. They are seen as demons by many ghost hunters and paranormal professionals. Usually, if you have one of these in your home then something negative is going on.

Shadow phenomenon can be seen in many forms from a solid black silhouette to a black mist. They can also shape shift or use whatever form they want.

In my experience they usually take on the form of loved ones and or animals. Remember that these are considered dangerous as not so nice things usually accompany them.

Alright back to my story. As I have told you already, we had many things happen in that house. Let's explore a few more occurrences shall we.

One night as a teenager of about 13 years of age I and a friend who would have been about 14 were there alone as usual. Don't worry the neighbors were all home and there was nothing to worry about really in that day and age.

The neighborhood was called Little Missouri. It was 10 suburban blocks of family oriented neighbors who all knew each other or grew up together in Missouri.

Dad was talking night classes at the local community college and working in the day so he could better himself. Anyway, my friend was talking to her boyfriend on the phone and I was practicing the flute. She turned to me and asked me to cook her some eggs.

I walked into the kitchen and put the cast iron skillet on the burner and turned it on. Click, click it was on. I walked to the refrigerator and took out two eggs and returned to the stove. I lightly oiled the skillet and cracked the eggs.

As I am standing there cooking I begin to get a very uneasy feeling on the right side of me. To the right was the hallway leading to the bathroom and bedrooms as well as the Office. The hallway was black as pitch at night. Feeling uneasy I walked back into the living room. What happened next unnerved me a bit.

I heard the stove click off.

This is not a fabricated story, nor am I joking. I heard the stove CLICK off.

A little information about the stove, it made a clicking noise every time you turned the knob. It clicked twice for on as it lit the pilot light and once for off. My curiosity got the better of me and I walked back into the kitchen only to discover my worst fears had come true.

The stove was in fact off.

I mean the burner was off and the knob had been turned to the off position.

I wasn't yet panicking. I was more interested in finding out what had happened. Was there a problem with the knob?

My father being a carpenter and taking me on many jobs, I think, brought out the problem solver in me. As I stood there trying to figure out what had actually happened I pulled off the knob looking for a spring or something to give me a clue.

Nothing was wrong, nothing. I decided to turn the burner back on. I stood there and nothing happened. I left it on and returned to the living room.

Again, I hear the click. Ok now I am beginning to think something weird is going on. I rush back into the kitchen and again the stove is off.

Hey fun idea, why don't I turn it back on and off again. Then I can go into the living room and see what happens. Little did I know that stupid stove would turn it-self back on just as I enter the living room.

Didn't see that coming did you? Yeah shocking!

Returning into the kitchen, I turn the burner back on and off again and return to the living room. I will get this figured out I thought. Again I hear the stove, but this time it turns on then off again.

Ok what is going on? This cannot be happening. The stove came with the house and was very old, but in all these years it had never once failed.

It was a very nice stove with a grill in the center and pie oven on the side. Again I check the dial and nothing seems to be wrong. I turn it on and back off again and stand there. That was a smart idea right?

I'm standing there waiting and watching for a reaction from the stove with that creepy feeling growing on my right again. It was growing seriously intense and all I wanted to do was get out of that room, but I was determined to figure this stove out and stand my ground.

All of a sudden an apparition, ghost, come out of the hallway. It was in full color. The apparition had on white shoes and it stepped into the kitchen with me.

I was so frightened that all I can really remember about him was that he was wearing white shoes and dark clothes.

I let out a scream that should have caused the paint peel off the ceiling. I wasn't about to stick around to see that happen. I ran out of the kitchen through the dining room and into the living room. I was near the foyer now.

My friend was sitting there talking on the phone. She stood up and hung up the phone. She ran out the door behind me. She must have understood by my scream that hanging out in the house alone was not a good idea.

Running out the door, she shuts the door behind her. This would have been a great idea had it been a real person chasing us. Who knows maybe it was a good idea in any situation.

The door locked automatically when you shut it and neither one of us had the key on our person as we had not planned to leave. My Dad was at night school and the neighbor who had a spare key was not home. Go figure.

I stood by the mailbox at the edge of the road lamenting over the key being inside. Not really worried about what had just happened. Yes I was a little shaken up but I would have been fine to return inside after a few minutes.

Meanwhile, she sat on the porch with her back on the screen door and the wooden door behind it. The lights were on in the house and it was dark outside in spite of the street lights.

As I stood there looking at the house and my friend I could see something happening inside the house near the front door. There was movement of some sort. The curtain made it somewhat blurry.

Suddenly I saw something strange coming up in the window of the door. It had an exaggerated round and huge head with a skinny neck and two hands. I couldn't yell for her to run. I have somewhat of a delayed reaction to startling events and this certainly was one of them.

What happens next I am sure the other girl still has nightmares about some twenty-five years later.

She stood up and ran so hard and fast that I could not catch up with her and I was the faster runner between us. We ran around to the next street over and briskly walked down the street talking about what had just happened.

We decided to head back to the house, but she had decided she would stand near the mailbox with me this time. I think that was a wise choice.

When we arrived back to my home, we noticed that the neighbor was finally home. Thank God. We asked her husband to please check out the house so we could return inside. My friend stayed outside and I headed in behind him.

Nothing at all was in the house. It was about 9:30pm and my dad came home a few minutes after the neighbor inspected the house.

We ran out and bombarded him with what had happened. He was sure that someone had been in the house and went about inspecting the house. He also found no evidence that anyone other than us had been in the house.

Shocking right?

Interview with Nyomie M.

I was living in a small town in Louisiana. I was a child of about 10 years old. I was there with my sister and with family and friends.

We were sitting on stools and they would move. Then it would stop us quickly. I believe that it was just in case we would fall. It was as if it was trying to keep us safe but play with us.

We named it Elmo just so we could talk to it and thank it and also try to understand what was happening. Like what was that? Elmo. Oh ok.

I believe in God and I believe in the paranormal. I have had other things happen there as well. I was sitting in the chair with a scarf and something would push us back.

I also saw a woman in a white dress. I thought I was crazy at first but when I realized that others were seeing these things as well I began to understand and now I know.

Chapter Five

For twenty-two years many things happened in that house. The majority of the things that happened were easily explained as black shadows and strange sounds.

My dad saw many black shadows hovering around the walls. Let me quickly tell you about a couple of situations that happened years later. This doesn't involve a black shadow but does seem relevant as to what I have already discussed.

My step brother Jimmy used to hang out with me a lot. We had mutual friends and enjoyed the same things in life. He was a few years older than me but that was alright. His best friend, John, was my boyfriend.

One day my brother was over and he and I were talking about the old boiler heaters and the fact that he had never seen one before. He was older than me and I thought that was a little weird. I took him downstairs into the basement and showed him our boiler and explained how my dad said it worked.

He was sitting on the steps listening to me when the door behind him slammed shut. He jumped up and run up the steps and no one was there. We talked about it after and I was sure there was someone there who closed the door as I saw a man in dark pants with white shoes on close that very same door. I was looking straight at him. Again, he said there was nothing. Remind you of another situation in that hallway?

Another time a friend of mine was staying the night. At that point I was a bit of a rebel. I was listening to very heavy metal music and was into the macabre. We had a séance in my closet of which we were trying to contact a recently dead metalist.

Sitting in the closet with one candle as the mechanism of conveyance for yes and no answers we concentrated and asked questions. Believe it or not we received answers. Later that night when we went to bed something happened.

I had a record player in my room. In the middle of the night, very nearly midnight, my record dropped and turned on. You could hear its obvious clicks and it even lowered the needle. It skipped all the way to the last song which began with Winston Churchill's speech and ended with a song called 2 Minutes to Midnight.

That was an impossible thing to happen. Sure the record could have fallen because of a weak part or defective something or another, but to lift the needle and put it on the last song and to start the record player required some strength and agility because of the type of switch it had.

This scared my friend so bad that we slept on the sofas in the living room. She refused to go back into my room for some time. I suppose we deserved that one since we had done a séance in my closet.

These are just the highlights of the things that happened in this house. I could go on for days and I might give a few flash backs later on in the journal if I feel the need to do so.

I always kept animals and sometimes they would alert to something. The kitchen was a hot spot in that house as it would seem by what I have already told you.

In the summer of 1996 I would leave that house and never return or even look back.

I believe everything I experienced in that house only prepared me for what was yet to come. It made me stronger and less afraid and I am thankful for that.

It is not to say that I do not get scared, because I do on occasion become quite afraid. You will understand more of what I am talking about as you continue to read the following chapters.

Different- A short story by Kristian V.

Ever since I can remember, I have seen some people turn into bats and others into wolves.

I myself say and eat brains. I am Tom the zombie.

I'm not able to talk to humans because they always run away, so I stay home.

My friend Mac the mummy says that I'm different.

I tell him he is too.

That's my life every day, so thanks humans.

Chapter Six

I moved to a small city in southeast Louisiana. My father moved here a few weeks later. I believe that my dad was a sort of magnet for the paranormal. Sure there were strange feelings and creepy happenings before he came, but wherever he was it seemed to be that much more unnerving.

The house we bought was owned by a school teacher. Before her it was the home of her aunt and uncle who worked at the local paper mill and chemical plant we were told. They were the only owners of the house before us.

Next door was the empty house of her best friend. That house was sold a few days after we bought ours. The family who bought the house next door offered us a small sum to sell our house to them but we refused. The teacher was the only one left between the two houses and she was in a local nursing home. Five years after being placed there she would succumb to age.

The house is a spacious three bedroom arts and craft style home. The ceilings are nine feet high and each of the rooms is 20x24 or 18x16. There are eleven rooms. The only exceptions are the measurements of the bathroom and office which, by the way, was the breakfast room.

You just have to love these old houses. All the charm of the south is in them. Oh, did I forget to mention the 28 windows and 18 doors? Yes, I am serious twenty-eight windows that are 108 inches wide and eighteen doors of which only two lead outside. It's a lot of painting trim work every time I re-paint. Forget cleaning the windows.

The house has a mother-in-laws apartment behind it which is a one bedroom and very nice size efficiency. All this sits on just over two acres in the middle of the city. I use city loosely.

Yes it is a city, but barely. At one time there was more property, but the teacher sold fifty feet off the back and the neighbor lady did as well.

Have you ever walked into a place and felt a weird vibe? Yeah, this house does that to everyone. From the beginning I did not want to be alone in this house nor did I want to look out the windows because I felt I would see something I didn't really want to see.

I was brave and walked around the yard and even lay in the back yard under the sun reading books or communing with nature. Upon arriving at this house we began some much needed repairs and clean up.

We ripped up carpet and repainted the inside as well as the outside. The house had sat empty with the windows open for five years and there were a few things to do to make it livable again.

Yard work was greatly needed. There were wonderful gardens that were large and full of beautiful flowers, but you couldn't see them for the weeds and bushes that had overgrown.

Once the yard work was done we began planting flowers and fruit trees as well as berry bushes. My father had a real green thumb. He had worked at a greenhouse at some point in his youth and picked up some knowledge on different plants and how to grow them. I guess it didn't hurt that he grew up farming and working as a carpenter either.

Nighttime was something different in that house, not that day time was much better. When night fell I was usually busy with school work and talking to my friends in chat rooms on the internet.

Sometimes you could hear a tapping as if a quarter was being tapped on a glass. I would chalk that sound up to some animal or wind or any natural sound that I just could not see at the time.

I am very much a skeptic and do not give into irrational thought very easily. When I hear a sound I cannot explain I do not believe that it was a ghost just because I cannot explain it or didn't see what caused that sound.

One night I was sitting at my computer at about ten o'clock in the evening and I felt a cool breeze pass by me as if you had opened the refrigerator on a hot day and the cold came rushing out at your feet, but it was during those wonderfully mild days where you do not use the heater nor the air conditioner and not a window need be opened.

I looked around and saw nothing and couldn't quite figure out the breeze although I had had this type of experience before, when I was praying years prior. Anyway, being a skeptic I shrugged it off and a little while later I decided to go to bed.

I turned off the lights and headed towards the bed when I looked over to the sofa in the living room. The sofa was sitting in front of the window and light was seeping in from the street light and the security light I had installed in the side yard for safety.

The thing that creped me out was not being able to see in my own driveway, so I had it installed. What I saw in the living room was a bit frightening.

There was a man sitting right smack dab in the middle of the sofa. I know he was there because I could see his silhouette. He had on a baseball hat. I clicked on the light, startled. No one was there.

I had just seen the clear black silhouette of a full grown man wearing a baseball hat and he wasn't really there. That made me nervous.

I went to bed and crawled under the covers making sure to tuck in all the covers all the way around me and my family. My son, at the time, refused to sleep in his own bedroom. I will give more details about that a little later.

As the days clicked by I barely gave that night another thought. I must have chalked it up to my imagination or exhaustion by this point.

Life continued on as it had always with me in school and working, my husband working and my son in school. My dad was retired and spent most of his time drinking coffee and chatting with his friends sitting at a local eatery. But the strange experiences soon returned.

Continuing to hear sounds and feel cool breezes something came to mind. I had bought a video camera for vacation use and to video my son when he was a baby. I decided to set it up and let it run all night long. We had no inside animals so there would only be interference if we did something and that was a plus.

I set it up between my dad's room and mine and put it on night vision. I hit record and went to bed. When I got up the next day I made everyone breakfast and decided to review the tape.

Of everything which was recorded I captured only the tapping that I would hear in person on occasion and still hear it to this day. Nothing visual appeared. I was somewhat disappointed but also relieved.

Again putting it out of my mind I continued on with life and one night I decided to sit up and watch a history show. The strange thing about this was there was not a single woman on this history show. The group of experts was made up of all men and not a single woman voice sounded on the TV.

The volume was very low and I could barely hear what they were talking about, but I was very interested. Maybe it was because I studied Anthropology in college with a minor in Sociology. I have a background in Psychology and Theology as well so naturally I thought I would like it.

While watching the show all of a sudden I heard a woman's voice sound out. It seemed to be about 3 feet in front of me and that puts it about 3 feet away from the TV as well. I turned my head to the right to look in the direction from where it came. I heard the woman's voice say "I am here ".

This did not scare me or unnerve me. I was in fact perplexed by it. I did not recognize the voice. But if you believe that you can tell anything about someone by their voice, she sounded like she was about 30 years old and northern. Her voice was so clear and loud. I could hear her over the TV. It was if she were standing in that spot talking to me in a normal voice.

I pondered what I heard for a few moments and listened for any other sounds even from the outside to no avail. There were no other sounds. I couldn't help but wonder why she said 'I am here' and not I'm here. It almost didn't sound normal or natural to say it like that.

Deciding that this was not the wind or a branch scratching on the window or anything I could explain let alone understand, I woke my dad up. I asked him had he heard a woman's voice in the living room with me. He assured me that he had not heard her at all. As I was leaving his room he said one last thing to me. "If you hear something like that again, ask it what it wants".

My father had always told me that things like this existed and not to ever to be afraid of these things. I would have never thought of asking it questions. I didn't even want these things to happen to me.

Soon I would come to terms with the fact that some people are meant to have these things happen to them and some were not. Not that this makes me feel any better.

Since hearing the woman's voice I have heard my name called numerous times. My husband and son have experienced the same thing with hearing their names being called.

My son comes to me so regularly that is has become quite annoying and I am at the point of telling him to assume that I did not call him and continue on with whatever he is doing. I can always go to him if I need him for something.

When it happens to my husband it isn't as often but it does happen. He also believes that it is me calling his name. This leads me to believe that since I heard a woman's voice and my husband and son also hear what sounds like my voice then there must be a female entity of some sort hanging around.

Interview with Ken and Bonnie B.

I was on the computer in an AOL chat room called Soul mate Reader at 2am.

Bonnie, my wife, was sleeping.

All of a sudden I hear "OUCH! Why did you do that?"

A book had fallen off the shelf and hit Bonnie in the head. The same thing happened again and this time left a lump.

Another time Bonnie was sitting there and a box fan lifted up into the air and sat back down again.

Chapter Seven

In this house, my experiences became so numeral that I couldn't take it any longer. I moved out. Finding a little house across town next to a church seemed ideal. I would be safe next to the church I thought.

That was my first mistake, believing that it would not be the same as at the other house. I had experiences in the house I grew up in and again in the house we moved into, now it was going to stop just because I moved? Yeah, right.

The house was a cute three bedroom house. It was all wood paneling throughout the entire house with hardwood floors and cabinets. The only exception was one of the back bedrooms. This room was painted and had tiled floors.

The house had three access doors. One was in the living room and another one was on the carport as well as one in the kitchen leading out to the back yard.

The living room and dining rooms were open concept while a small wall separated the kitchen from the living room. The hallway was long and dark. As you walked down the hall to the left was a bedroom and to the right the bathroom.

If you continue on to the end of the hallway you find the other two bedrooms one on the left and one on the right.

The one on the right was the painted room and it was at the back of the house.

A family member was staying with me for a little while and he decided that he wanted that room for his own because it had the most closet space. Not only was there a regular closet but there was one of those small crawl in closets you see in the older homes sometimes. He was in love with this room.

Since it was painted he bought some stencils and a small can of paint and painted a border of green ivy around the room. It looked very nice. He never slept a single night in that room though.

Every morning I would wake up to go to work and find him sleeping on the sofa. I would ask him what was going on and he would tell me he could hear monkeys in his room. I would tell him I was sorry and to try again the next night. He would try but he could not under any circumstance sleep in that room.

After a couple of months of this he was telling a friend about it and his friend asked if we could all go in that room and just sit a while. We did just that. As we sat there talking about things and looking through his trunk of items we all began to hear the sound of monkeys.

No joke we could hear the sound of monkeys. It was not a sound being made by the wind. It was monkeys, clearly monkeys. If you have ever been to the zoo then you know that is an unmistakable sound.

Our friend opened the window explaining about amphitheaters and how they carry sound and that the sound could be generated a few houses away but somehow be concentrated on this spot and opening the window he could get a better clue as to where it was coming from.

We stuck our heads outside and there were no sounds at all. Not even crickets. Nothing, no noise could be heard. Back inside with our heads and you could hear monkeys.

One stuck his head out and the other kept it in and still the sound was inside but not outside. Our friend decided someone was playing a joke on us.

He took his 357 revolver, he was in law enforcement, and walked the property and around the house inside and out. Nothing turned up, but you could still hear the monkeys in only that room. Every nook and cranny was inspected for recorders and or anything else, but nothing presented itself.

Our friend offered for us to stay the night with him and my family member went because he was afraid. I did not because he lived in the country twenty miles away and I had to go to work early and it was very late already. I woke up the next morning and went to work.

One day my boss asked me how did I like living in that house? I found that strange. I said it was a nice house and asked him how he knew I lived there. He told me that he had seen my car there and was wondering how it was going. I assured him that everything was peachy and he seemed to be honestly concerned.

The next day was my off day and I decided to stay in bed. Even though I was awake I just wanted to relax a few more minutes before I got up and started cleaning. My family member would be home from his weekend in the country later and I would need to get some things done before he came home.

As I lay in bed with my bedroom door wide open I saw a man wearing black pants and black shiny shoes step out of my family member's room. He paused in the hallway then disappeared. I just lay there hardly breathing. There was someone in the house.

I did not hear anything at all. After a few minutes of gaining my composure, and a little bravery as well, I got up and walked the entire house. I checked all doors and windows. Everything was locked. There was no one in the house with me. Either I had seen a ghost or I was going crazy.

My family member came home and I told him what happened and he told me he was afraid there and he had been touched by something and hadn't told me because he did not want to frighten me. I was admittedly a bit scared.

Anyway, I went to work the next morning and saw a man out back. Thinking it was the garbage man I hurried out there to give him some more garbage but there was no one there.

I told my boss and he said that it was his uncle and he was surprised that after a year and a half that was the first time I had seen him. I told him that I had thought I had seen someone before walk through or up the stairs but never placed much value on it because I was too busy. He asked me again how it was going in my house.

This time I asked him to please tell me why he kept asking me this question. He broke down and said there are things that people in this town do not talk about and my house is one of them.

I said to him 'ok you know I am neither from this town nor state so please tell me what you know or something, anything really and I will tell you something about it as well.'

He began telling me that there had been a couple who lived in the house and one night someone had come in and murdered them both while they were in bed sleeping. No one was ever caught or convicted of the crime, but the room was so bloody that they had to paint the room white and tile the floor because the blood wouldn't completely wash away. He even went so far as to tell me where that room was located in the house.

He was right. That room had been the painted room. When I got home I called the man whom I paid for the house and asked him and his words made me shiver.

He told me that it happened before he owned the house and that as much as he rented it no one ever stayed more than a couple of months claiming it to be haunted. I hung up with him and had a conversation with my dad and husband as well as my family member.

Again not being one to allow fear to overtake me, we decided to stay in the house. One night my family member now being afraid to sleep at night at all, and spending as much time as possible away from the house, asked me if we could make a Ouija board and try to contact whatever spirit that was there. He wanted to see if we could help it move on because he was very afraid to be there.

He would rather walk all around town all day than to stay there. We lived just on the outskirts of town and he had to walk some three miles to anything. We had no neighbors, just a church next door.

Reluctantly, after my previous experiences with an Ouija board, I decided that if it made him feel better we would try it.

He and I sat down with some small bits of paper and an ink pen and began to write letters, numbers and key words found on the witches boards. Once we were done we affixed them to a small end table about the size of a real Ouija board and got a juice glass out of the kitchen.

He put two fingers from each had on his side of the glass and I did on the other side as well. We closed our eyes and relaxed. Concentrating on the questions we began to ask if anyone was there with us. Slowly the glass began to move.

The glass slid back and forth and back and forth gaining momentum with every pass and return. We both opened our eyes and looked at each other and the glass stopped. I was sure he was moving the glass and he was positive I was.

What happened next literally proved my innocence and reluctance to even participate in something like that again.

We closed our eyes and began to concentrate again while asking if anyone was there. I took my fingers off of the glass before the glass started to move and opened my eyes and just watched.

The glass began to move and he thought he would be smart and catch me moving the glass and opened his eyes to see my hands behind my head fingers laced as to show I was not touching the glass.

His hands came up to his mouth as fast as he opened his eyes and he began to cry out of fright. The glass then picked up off of the table about six inches and shot straight across the room without an arch and smashed into the door that was about twelve feet away with such a force that it left a dent in the wooden door and shattered the glass.

In my entire life I had never seen sheer terror as I saw at that moment in the eyes of my family member. At that point I began to explain to him that this is why one does not do these things because they are dangerous.

He told me that he could have sworn it was me. I told him that I believed it was him and that is why I took my fingers off and laced them behind my head. I was not expecting the glass to pick up and fly into the door either.

I explained that these boards are not a toy and should not be played with as if they were a toy. He claimed that because they were being sold as a toy in the stores that he only half believed that there was something to it.

After informing him that one's homemade boards are more powerful because you put your own energy into them and that it should never happen again, he understood and asked if we were going to be alright.

I reassured him that we were and there was nothing to worry about. We needed to close the gate we opened and never reopen it again. He agreed and we did close the gate.

He never asked me again to do that at all nor did he have much interest in the paranormal after that. As I said before, I believe some are meant for it and some are not. Nothing else ever happened to him that I am aware of. We moved back into the other house soon after that incident.

Before we moved, I had a dream. I dreamed another family member was visiting me and him. We were in the back bedroom talking. She turned and walked down the hall with him following behind her and me pulling up the caboose. As we walked down the hall she continued to talk and he was answering her.

It was evening and very dark outside as I could see out the window from the room we were entering. The lights were on in the house and the amber-caramel glow was very pretty on the wood flooring and walls.

We turned to walk out the front door when I stopped and turned to see a man with straight dark hair sitting in an arm chair facing the kitchen which was facing away from me. I could not see his face. He was wearing a long sleeve button down shirt. It was neatly pressed and white in color.

I walked over to him and knelt down beside the chair and put my head in the bend of his elbow and he wrapped his arm ever so gently around my head. I felt very much in love with this man. I did not even want to leave his arms because of the way I was feeling.

I had noticed that the door had shut when I turned around and I wasn't worried at all about opening it. I just wanted to stay right there in his arms.

When I woke up out of this dream, I called my family member to talk to her. My dad taught me that sometimes we dream about someone because they need some help or something is going on. As we were talking that morning, she began to tell me about her dream.

I listened and was excited she was talking about dreams because I wanted to tell her about mine. As I sat there on my sofa and listened to her dream I couldn't believe my ears. She was telling me my dream.

Every detail was the same with the exception that she saw it from her perspective and I saw it from mine.

She saw the man in the chair. She saw me turn and go to him then the door shut. She was standing on the outside of the door with my other family member beating the door down trying to get in to get me out.

Boy was I surprised when she told me her dream.

I asked her if she believed in more than one person having the same dream and she said yes that she did but she believed that if two or more people had the same dream then there was a very good reason for it.

People do not just happen to dream the same dream at the same time as the other.

I came away from my conversation with her feeling confused and yet satisfied that someone else had the same dream as I did.

All of a sudden I felt not so alone in my paranormal happenings. I do believe that this is a journey that we who are afflicted by the paranormal must take, for the most part, alone.

There will be help from time to time. This help could come from something that you read or saw on TV or it could come from a conversation with a friend, but it is meant for us to come to our own understanding of what we are experiencing.

Interview with Stacey A.

It came out of the closet. Like most kids I was prone to see them. I was about seven or eight years old.

I saw a human shaped black figure come out of my closet. As it approached my bed I could see it had a meat cleaver. It stuck the meat cleaver into the head board above my head about 5 or 6".

I thought it was a nightmare and rolled over and went back to sleep. When I woke up in the morning the meat cleaver was actually there.

My mom saged the house and got rid of it. There were no discerning facial features with this thing.

We lived near Chicago. I hadn't been doing anything that day just playing outside. My mom saw the knife. Others were aware of what had happened as well.

I strongly believe in the paranormal now. I believe in God, but not that there is just one. I believe that there has got to be another power balancing it out. I believe that I have suppressed abilities.

Chapter Eight

Returning to the former home that was some two miles away, we once again began to settle back into our daily routine.

Yes indeed, everything was returning to normal. Normal, WOW! That is a loaded word.

Normal is something common place or that happens regularly to the majority of people. Normal for me is not the mainstream normal however.

Up until this very point in this journal I have been giving you background information on me as well as some minor experiences.

One thing I haven't mentioned yet is that I formed a paranormal group about fifteen years ago. The name of this group has been newly named Global Paranormal Society – GPS.

I have also been trying to work out how I am going to tell you all the experiences that I have had.

I have decided that I will not tell you everything in this journal. I will only highlight my experiences with you this time.

The next installments will give you more and more personal experiences that I have had as well as the group. I will also explain more terms and have photographs.

Before I go any farther I am going to define a few terms for your better understanding as to what I personally am referring to when I talk about things.

Some handy terms:

Apparition – Energy that materializes and can be seen.

Cold Spot – A specific area that has a cooler temperature localized to that area.

Demon – A non-human of Angelic origin that interacts with humans for malicious intentions.

Ghost – Apparition

Ghost Box – *Frank's Box* – *Spirit Box* – A digital radio that has been altered to sweep through the channels as to not stop on any. Spirits allegedly can use this devise to speak in an audible voice.

Haunting – Location having paranormal activity.

Poltergeist – In German literally means noisy ghost. Objects move and people see false apparitions. This is believed to be brought on by adolescent females going through puberty.

It is common in homes with teen females but can happen with males as well. It is a subconscious occurrence and the victim has no idea it is their rapidly changing brainwaves that may be the culprit.

Now back to the journal.

There is a funny thing about this home I live in. It was purchased in the late spring / early summer of 1996. I loved the house from the moment that I saw it.

It was large enough for two families. The house was built in 1935 in the Arts and Crafts style. The ceilings are nine feet high and every corner, window, door and wall has large yet elegant molding.

Sunlight is abundant with its twenty-eight windows. The spacious home boasts eighteen hardwood doors and hardwood floors throughout the entire dwelling.

A closed in veranda sprawls across the front of the house while a small adequate closed in porch perches in the back of the house just off of the kitchen.

Take a few steps down the covered breezeway steps and you have arrived at the one bedroom mother-in-law apartment.

It is just the perfect size for a single person or a couple without children. That entire splendor sits on just over two acres in the city.

I have only two neighbors and one of them does not live in their house. This house is in front of mine.

The other house can only be seen from the front and not from the back. The grounds once boasted beautiful flower gardens but when we moved in they had to be cleaned out.

The house sat empty for five years and the yard was overgrown.

Trees line the property and you cannot see the road from three sides. It is very quiet and very private.

When we first moved in we came in and cleaned the house out as it was full of the previous owners clothing and some furniture items.

She was a school teacher as I said before and her uncle had worked at the local mill. Some repairs had to be done as well as repainting. All the carpet had to go.

We remodeled the apartment and rented it out to a young lady who worked at the bank.

She only stayed about a month and a half. She was never home. I don't believe she was comfortable there. The apartment was nice, clean and comfy.

It would be another twelve years before we would remodel again and rent it out yet again. The man we rented it to would stay in the main house claiming he didn't feel right in there but when he was sleeping it didn't bother him.

Interview with Amanda M.

It was about 5 years ago. I was about 31 years old. My family and another family were rooming together.

My husband and my friend's husband had just left for work. I was fully awake. I am not crazy. I saw what I saw.

I only had things happen in that place. I had never had anything happen anywhere else. I was lying in the bed and I saw a woman wearing a white dress come into my room.

Another time I saw her pass by my door. I believe in God and the paranormal.

Other people saw the same things as me. Many other things happened in the house like a man was standing outside that wasn't really there and the very loud bangs that scared the kids.

That was a crazy place to live.

Chapter Nine

From the start of living in this house I wasn't comfortable, as I have said before. I was afraid of looking out the windows. Crazy I know, but I just knew something was out there.

During the day I was unstoppable. I would roam all over the yard with no problems. I would even layout in the sun all day on some days.

I loved to lie out and read my books in the private back yard. It was a rare occasion during the day that I felt as though I was being watched.

We had moved into the house in June and it was late for planting, so when spring came we were excited. We went down to the local nursery and purchased several fruit trees such as: Fig, kumquats, lemon, grapefruit, oranges, and tangerines.

Muscadines, blueberries and raspberries were also purchased and planted. Everything took root and started to grow very fast.

The trees bore fruit, albeit not a lot, and were ready for harvest in the fall. The following season, to our surprise, the trees grew quite a bit and were heavily laden with fruits.

Excited, I took my digital camera out to take photographs of the fruit and the trees. I began by taking pictures of the sweet orange tree and moved on to the fig.

After that were the lemon tree and the not so sweet orange tree. Next I began taking photographs of the grapefruit tree. I then moved on to the tangerine tree and kumquat trees.

As I was walking back by the trees in the direction from which I came, I became overwhelmingly aware of something to my left.

I turned and walked back to the grapefruit tree. I stopped to listen, no sound. The feeling grew stronger and I began to grow more and more afraid with each passing second.

I snapped a photo in the direction that the feeling seemed to emanate from, waited a second and snapped another. My house is built on a hill and the back part of the house is up on stilts to keep it level.

The roof of the mother-in-law's apartment is at the floor level of the kitchen in the back of the main house.

After snapping the photos I quickly ran into the house and uploaded the photographs onto my computer for analysis. When reviewing the last two photographs that I took, I couldn't believe my eyes.

The second photo was normal without any unusual anomalies at all, but it was the first photo that I would immediately have to send to various persons to get their opinions on as well.

I am just going to come out and say it without dragging this on. What I captured in the first photo when I had that overwhelming feeling was, in my opinion, an Indian.

A Native American Indian wearing a breast plate and earrings. He also appeared to have a feather in his hair and was holding a staff in his right hand.

This was beyond belief. I sent this photo to my cousin without telling her what I saw and she also picked up on the exact same Indian that I had.

My cousin also picked up on something I had not noticed in the photograph. I guess I was too emotional from seeing the Indian.

It was something much more sinister. She saw a second figure. Evidently I hadn't noticed it because I was so wrapped up in seeing the Indian in the photograph.

The image was that of a hooded figure. Imagine if you will all of the imagery of the grim reaper that you have ever seen and you have something to use as a representation of what could be seen in the picture.

It was standing to the left of the Indian, or on the right side of the photo. It was wearing a black hooded robe. You could see its face and it appeared to be a skull. It was also a little taller than the Indian.

Now I was really freaked out. I mean come-on, I was already uneasy or uncomfortable there and now I was beginning to feel very frightened.

Yes I was naturally curious as to what they wanted and to why they had made their presence known to me, but at the same time I wondered if they were a bad omen or something to that nature.

Now I could no longer ignore the shadows I had grown accustom to seeing. I couldn't ignore the sound of talking at a distance or the mists that would wisp by. I realized beyond doubt that these were not just a play of light or imagination.

I decided that there was no need to be afraid after I had a talk with my father. He explained to me that things we cannot understand, unless they are revealed to us, are all around us all the time. Angels, Demons, Ghost, Energies and so on and so forth.

My Dad told me to keep an open mind and try to understand. He also told me that he had been trying to train me to see these things and understand them better from a very young child. He, himself, dreamed dreams and could see things that others could not see.

He got this gift, he said, from his mother. She had Native American blood running through her veins. My Grandmother 'knew' things. She could also interpret dreams.

The things that my grandmother was able to do in the old ways are now days called witchcraft. Although more and more people are opened up to it, it is still incorrect labeling and the knowledge of how to do these things is rapidly being lost with each generation.

My Grandmother was born in the late 1800's and my father was the last child born to my grandparents.

I was my father's last child as well. He would look at me and smile. This would sometimes make me feel weird because I didn't understand why, so I asked him one day when I was about 12.

He said that he knew why his mother died two months before I was born. When I asked why he said that it was because I had to be born and that I was her reincarnated.

I thought that was weird and didn't place much significance on it until later when he explained further to me what he meant by that.

My father had a long conversation with me one day and told me that he honestly believed that I was his mother reborn. He said that, even though I resembled his sister more, he just knew.

He went on to explain to me that he will sit and watch me and see that I have had no instruction with something and I seem to understand what I need to do. For example, crocheting, sewing, or painting.

I painted a painting once of a sandy beach with palm trees and a bridge. When I showed it to my father said he would be right back. When he came home he showed me a piece of sheetrock that had a painting on the other side. When he turned it over I was astonished.

The painting on the other side was that of a sandy beach with palm trees and a bridge. My grandmother had painted it. I had never seen this painting and had never been told about it.

My father could attest to that because he had it stored away from everyone and no one ever knew he even had it much less know she painted it.

He sat me down and asked me if I now understood what he was referring to when he said he believed I was his mom. I did see his point and was slightly freaked out about it too.

Don't get me wrong, my dad didn't believe in reincarnation but he wasn't so closed minded that he couldn't believe that God could allow me to understand the things his mom did without being taught them.

Anyway, back to my experiences in the house after that small piece of background information.

Chapter Ten

I still live in this house today. As I sit here writing this all down I can't help but think back on some of the things that happened and have not presented themselves in a while. I do not want them to return, but find them interesting.

I remember sitting here at the dining table with my friend who was staying with us for a few months. We were playing a game with her two daughters, my son and another friends two children.

It was evening and about 7pm. Our husbands had been working all day and had not come home yet. This was normal practice for us. We were home all day cleaning and cooking. When the children came home we made sure their homework was done and they were fed and bathed.

This was a Friday night and we made sure that we did extra things with them like play games or do crafts. Yes we did things during the week but Friday night was more special.

Anyway we were sitting there and all of a sudden a super loud BOOM happened that sounded like it came from the back porch. Our back porch was closed in and had 2 screen doors and one wooden door, but it did not sound like either one of them.

What we imagined happened was that the industrial fan that was screwed to the window on the back porch had fallen. This was all or our thoughts at the time. My friend and I went to check it out but the fan was still attached to the window just as it had been for some 60 years or so.

To say the least we were perplexed. I have been in sonic boom situations and this was not one of them. We have a hobby airport and the nearest large airport is an hour and a half away.

It happened again and we were yet again unable to find the source of the disturbance. I have never heard such a loud noise again in this house.

I also remember the same friend and I were heading out the door to run down to the gas station for something and we left the kids inside with a couple of friends. As we were walking out to the car some movement to our right got our attention. We stopped at the nose of the car and watched.

Seeing nothing we just stood there another moment. A car came down the road and rounded the curve and the headlights shined into the tree line next to the driveway. The car was not parked in the driveway it was parked in front of the house.

We both saw a man in a jean jacket slip behind the trees. The car that was coming down the road was my husband and we immediately told him what we saw. My friend's husband and my husband shined their headlights from opposite sides of the tree line and there was no one there.

They walked the trees with flashlights and released the German shepherd guard dog and still found no one. Years later I would find an old Timex watch in that exact spot. Freaky!

I have seen something similar twice more. Once when I was down in the mother in laws apartment visiting with the renter upon leaving I saw a man in a jean jacket standing there between the truck and the tangerine tree. He just stood there looking at me.

I pretended that I did not see him and hurried up the stairs. I slammed the door and screamed for my husband. My husband and my friend's husband went looking for the man but found no one.

Another time my two baby German shepherds were in their kennel in the living room cutting up and looking at the window. Believing that it was an animal outside, I casually looked out the window.

Oh My! Why did I do that? There was a man in a hoodie standing there looking up into the window. I screamed and ran to my bedroom and got my husband up.

He ran outside in his underwear trying to find this man. It was around Christmas and even in the south it can get chilly, but that didn't faze my husband any. He was more concerned about the man that was looking up into our window.

Dare I say that he found no one? At this point my husband is beginning to believe that I need a doctor. He couldn't discount the many claims from various persons stating what they experienced at the home, but it was hard for him to believe since he was not experiencing anything.

I subsequently began to see more things in the house. Whatever this is it likes to mess with me when I am home alone. I do not like to take a shower when I am alone unless it is absolutely necessary. The creepiest feeling of someone on the other side of the curtain is bothersome.

Cleaning the house one day I was sweeping the hardwood floor in my living room and movement in my bedroom caught my eye. Knowing that only my son and I were home there should not have been movement in my room at all.

I looked up and saw a man facing me on my side of the bed. He hunched down in what I can only think of as an attack position with his hands on my bed. It was almost as if he was waiting for me to move to pounce on me. I bet he could have leaped my bed in a single bound.

Standing there and not showing fear nor was I backing down with my stare and he did the same to me. Soon my son got my attention and I glanced away for a split second and returning my eyes to the apparition beside my bed he shot off into the wall.

Getting the experience out of my mind will never happen. I remember the clothes he was wearing and his features. His eyes almost glowed in the darkened room. I have not seen him more than once again and that was not a pleasant thing at all.

Lying in bed asleep I was awoken by something. When I opened my eyes there was that same man over me. His face was about 10 inches away from my face.

This was something like you would see in a movie. Hovering over the victim at night while they sleep as it oppresses them around the clock.

I tried to scream but nothing would come out. I began to hit my husband and as he woke up the thing that I had hovering over me disappeared into thin air.

You might ask how I even saw this thing. I always sleep with a light on. This drives my husband insane but if the light is not on in my room as well as one in the kitchen I am not comfortable.

Don't laugh, it's true. I would rather see what is bothering me than to not see it. I picked this habit up as a child always needing a night light on in the bathroom.

Something else crazy, I can't sleep with the closet door open. I know that closets can be creepy but I have a real problem with the closet doors opening up in my house.

My pantry door in the kitchen would open up or shut so much that I took it off of the hinges. The pantry no longer exists due to remodeling but it is an experience in this house that will not be forgotten anytime soon.

Many people go their entire life and have zero experiences of the paranormal yet others are plagued with an overwhelming number of experiences. I am the latter.

My husband honestly believed that I was making these things up or was losing my mind as I stated before. He had not had any of these experiences in my house and believed that everything was normal. Then one day he didn't feel that way anymore.

My husband began to hear footsteps in the house in the middle of the night. He would get up and check the house and our son but find nothing wrong, nor anyone in the house that was not supposed to be there. We slept with our bedroom door open at the time because of our young son.

Many nights my husband would get up and check the house and one night he decided to sleep in the living room in the reclining chair so that he could figure things out better.

He believed that it was my son tiptoeing back to bed after going to the bathroom or maybe the house settling. We had no animals inside so it couldn't be them making human sounding footsteps.

As he slept in the chair waiting to hear the footsteps again he was suddenly rudely awakened but not by footsteps. He was awakened by being pulled backwards up and out of the chair and thrown onto the floor.

Amazingly enough, this man stayed in the house after this happened. His first real experience and it had to be violent with him. I guess it grew tired of my husband's nay saying or something.

My husband decided after that night that he wasn't going to sleep in the chair again though. Another night he was lying in bed and was pulled by the feet out of the bed.

Now at this point I believe that it has something against my husband. Honestly starting to worry about his safety here. My husband begins to hear me call his name when I am not calling him.

He also begins to get touched by an unseen force. He doesn't seem to be startled though. My husband seem to be more curious by whatever it is and maybe slightly angered because he doesn't know for sure what it is or wants.

One morning he was in the shower. I heard a huge thud from the shower. I ran in there to find my husband getting up from the floor. He told me that he was in the shower when he was picked up and thrown over the shower curtain and hit the door some 6 feet from the side of the tub.

He was wet and the shower curtain was in perfect place as though he was still in the shower. He went to work and soon forgot about the situation.

I have had things thrown at me in the house and even had things moved on me. There have been points I believed and accused my husband or son of moving something. I have always known where everything in my house was as I kept everything in its place.

I might lose a hairbrush only to find it in the bottom of a box; I hadn't opened in years, 3 months after it went missing. This happens way too often for me and has caused me to purchase multiple items that I shouldn't have had to buy.

Chapter Eleven

My son has had many experiences in the home as well. He has seen a man wearing brown clothes with brown skin in a tree outside of his window. He refused to sleep in his room until he was around 10. He now has two dogs that sleep in his room with him and he will not go to bed without them in there with him.

Whatever is in my house likes to single my son out at times and this not only makes me angry but my husband as well. It has prompted my husband to tell them that they need to leave my son alone.

My son has had brand new large bottles of laundry soap thrown at him. This of course caused us to laugh because what else are we supposed to do. We joked that it was trying to tell him something as we cleaned it up.

When it threw the class bottle of hot sauce at him I began to get angry. Don't mess with my son, period was the new attitude. They responded by throwing the same bottle at me.

One night our new neighbors came over to visit. They had been in their home for about a month or so and were being very friendly.

My husband came home from work with a bottle of soda for me. He placed it on the dining room table and sat down in the living room with us to chat. My living room and dining room are open concept and that leads me to what I am about to tell you next.

As we sat there talking the bottle lifted up off of the table and threw itself at the couple. It landed on the floor near them some twelve feet away from where my husband placed it.

My husband and I continued to talk without missing a beat and paid no attention to what had just happened other than my husband picking the bottle up and placing it on the coffee table.

Our neighbors stopped us from talking and asked us if we had seen that and we politely said we had but it was nothing for us. They freaked out a little and couldn't believe their eyes. They didn't come back after that and soon moved out of their house.

Another time my son's cat, which stays out side most of the time, came in to eat. I had to pee and he went into the bathroom with me looking for some petting. He lay down at my feet and all of a sudden the garbage can lifts up and comes down softly on the cats head 12 inches away and returns to its original position. The cat would not go back into the bathroom after that. I don't blame him.

During the time that the activity was at its greatest my health was seriously affected. I was experiencing one strange illness after another.

I thank God every day for all he has done for me. He healed me quickly. Without him I would not have made it through this time of the illnesses as well as the massive increase in paranormal activity in my home.

I was being bombarded by personal strife at the time as well which made my life a proverbial living hell. My husband and I believe that we discovered the source of the massive spike in activity as well as the violence that came with it.

The strife was not from my household, but from an overbearing and self-centered person who is as evil as the devil himself. They can only be held one of his many minions.

This person claims to love God in the same sentence that they badger and berate you. At the drop of a hat they will cut you down and threaten you with bodily harm because you did not answer the phone when they called even though you were in the shower at the time or some viable other reason.

This person is not worth mentioning for any reason other than for a reference as to the things that were happening in my house and with my health. We fully believe it was the sole reason it was so demonically active and violent at the time. This person was lashing out at us because of their own shortcomings and mental anguish due to their own self-inflicted poor personal choices of which we had no part in.

Someone had to be blamed and they were going to make sure it was not them. I do not believe it was that person exactly though. I believe that they harbor a demon or demons. If you research anything on demons you will see what I mean.

Also let this serve as a warning about whom you allow near you and your family because they could be carrying demons around with them and never realize they are being used or even, in some cases, ruled by the demons.

We were always good to this person and welcomed them into our home until one day my health and home life was more important to me and also to my family. We decided to become proactive in this situation and found the only source of grief was this person.

Since we have eliminated this person from our lives there is almost no activity in our home. I say almost because I don't know if it will ever come back. Lord I pray it doesn't. Since we completely cut this person off and out of our lives there is a peace and love in our home and for each other like we have never felt it before.

My relationship with my husband is so beautiful now. It is tender and caring. Before it was in a shambles because of the strife this person brought us.

I cannot begin to tell you or emphasize enough to you on the importance of being careful who you let around you and your family. Had we not rid ourselves of this evil person, I am sure we would not be in a good situation at this point.

We started going back to church recently also. This has helped us emotionally to heal and have a better understanding of Gods plan for our lives with him.

I am excited to finally be rid of the demons or entities that once plagued this house. No I was not a perfect person and did many things wrong, but *be very careful of the people around you because you never know when you are entertaining an angel or catering to a demon.*

Let me explain a few things here for you so that you can understand what I am talking about. I sure hope this helps you to avoid certain people and situations. Also don't forget God will have your back if you let him in.

To understand the Spirits and demonic presences we need to look at a few things. The parasite spirits can attach themselves to and draw energy from individuals. These spirits are often invited in or are just passing through.

Spirits are invited or attracted to a place, a thing, or a living person. They need energy to manifest in the physical world. A summoned spirit is attracted to a raise in the level of energy in a location by living beings.

Most will usually leave when the energy dissipates. Some find other places with energy to move on to. Usually they are harmful and intent on harming us and they pretty much leave us alone.

Parasites are like leaches. They attach themselves and feed on energy. It has been said of a parasite entity "The more they feed, the more they need."

Over time, by provoking strong emotional responses, a parasite can completely drain you. Given enough time this can lead to physical illness or an emotional breakdown.

Spirits, whether good or bad, can manipulate your energy. Your specific energy level as well as type of energy can influence your decisions. Your choices determine how you feel.

The Succubus and the Incubus, live off sexual energy. They like to keep you interested in sex or sexual things. You can become obsessed with what the spirit needs. This also drains you. This can lead to depression or mania and it happens over a short time period.

A parasite spirit is really dangerous. It is hard to get rid of them and will take time. You have to learn to adjust your energy to positive things in order for them to leave you.

Attachment is when an entity will watch and wait for a moment of weakness and literally attaches itself to you and works its way towards possession of the person.

Possession is when an entity breaks down your energy and will power and moves in. It actually takes possession of the person.

Spirits find a weakness or a door through their behavior or reckless behavior of the individual. A person who has done something that they have shame or guilt over is a good way for them to get in.

Here are some ways you might use to spot a demonically afflicted person.

Mental Changes include:

1. Changes in personality.

2. Someone active becomes antisocial.

3. Sleep patterns changes.

4. Changes in attitude and behavior.

5. Personal hygiene changes.

6. They are abusive and threatening for no reason.

7. They are violent.

8. They attempt humiliation.

9. They may be obsessed with sex.

10. They seem to have multiple personalities.

11. Blackouts.

Physical Changes include:

1. Changes in the eyes. Black and wild eyes are something to look out for.

2. Changes in their features.

3. Inhuman strength.

4. The sound of their voice could change.

5. Animals are scared of the person.

Outward Manifestations:

1. Objects move around by themselves.

2. Objects may disappear and be found in another location.

3. Knocking, banging or pounding may be heard throughout the house or in just one room.

4. Objects fly around as if they were thrown.

5. Knocks at the door but no one is ever there.

6. Growling.

7. Hear scratching.

8. Foul odors.

9. Heavy furniture moves on its own.

10. See people or dark shadows.

11. Doors and drawers open and close on their own.

12. Electrical appliances turn on or off.

13. Animals growl at something they see.

14. People have a feeling of being watched or that they are not alone.

15. People hear voices when no one is there.

16. People will often hear their name called. Sometimes, a couple will each think they heard the other calling them.

17. Physical attacks.

18. Psychological attacks like depression and anxiety

19. Levitation of objects or people.

MANIFESTATION is when the entity is invited in, intentionally or unintentionally.

Intentionally is trying to curse or bind someone, messing with the occult, trying to communicate with the dead, etc.

Unintentionally can be a negative thoughts, hatred toward, anger or rage, guilt or sadness, suicidal thoughts, reckless behavior.

INFESTATION is when the entity makes itself known to you. You have the feeling of being watched; hear knocks, whispers, and poltergeist activity.

OPPRESSION is when it is hard to sleep. You could also experience weaknesses, fears, guilt or grief. Also anxiety, anger or sadness, violence, self-hate and suicidal thoughts are common. You are being broken down so you are open to possession.

POSSESSION is when the entity has access to the body. At this point people may black out or watch from above while the entity has control of their body something like an out of body experience.

Paranormal is literally something that can't be explained by normal scientific explanation. Paranormal does not refer only to ghosts, although it is a very popular subject.

Paranormal can also refer to UFOs, Extra-terrestrials, and Psychic abilities, Cryptids such as Bigfoot or the Honey Island Swamp monster and the rouga-rou.

Parapsychology is the study of the paranormal. It is a branch of the Psychology school of thought and you can take classes on parapsychology in some colleges.

Just about every culture has beliefs about ghosts. Let's look at the bible since it is the most popular book of beliefs in the world.

1 Sam 28:13-15 shows us that something indeed does exist. Saul had the witch call up a spirit and she said she saw a divine being coming out of the earth. Saul asked her what was its form and she told him it was an old man in a robe. It was Samuel. Samuel, the spirit asked Saul why he disturbed him and bring him up. He told him that he was having trouble and needed to know what to do.

The book of Revelations 12:9 tells us that Satan and his angels were thrown down to earth. Mathew 10:1 Jesus called his disciples and gave them authority over unclean spirits to cast them out and heal every affliction.

Leviticus talks about mediums and spiritists. While Deuteronomy speaks of divination, psychics, charmers, witches, necromancers and consulters of spirits.

Even Jesus spoke about ghosts again in Luke 24 saying that ghosts don't have flesh and bones like he has.

Some schools of thought are to never mention them and they won't exist. Sure, to acknowledge them is to give them some sort of power or energy, but that isn't always negative. I believe that they do exist.

Acknowledgements

I give the highest honor and respect to God whose name is Jehovah. Thank you for waking me up every day and for believing in me. Without you nothing is possible.

Exodus 3:13-15

Then Moses said to God, "If I come to the people of Israel and say to them, 'The God of your fathers has sent me to you,' and they ask me, 'What is his name?' what shall I say to them?" God said to Moses, "I am who I am." And he said, "Say this to the people of Israel, 'I am has sent me to you.'"

God also said to Moses, "Say this to the people of Israel, 'The Lord, the God of your fathers, the God of Abraham, the God of Isaac, and the God of Jacob, has sent me to you.'

This is my name forever, and thus I am to be remembered throughout all generations.

Psalms 83:18

That men may know that thou, whose name alone is JEHOVAH, art the most high over all the earth.

Mathew 6:9-13

Our Father, which art in heaven, Hallowed be thy Name. Thy Kingdom come. Thy will be done in earth, as it is in heaven. Give us this day our daily bread. And forgive us our trespasses, as we forgive them that trespass against us. And lead us not into temptation, but deliver us from evil. For thine is the kingdom, the power, and the glory, For ever and ever. Amen.

Final Thoughts:

Whatever you believe, please use caution when dealing with things that you do not understand. My journey has taught me that not everything is what it seems to be and dangers do truly exist. Some unseen force is out there working against the good people of this world and they will not stop even once we give into them. Enjoy life, but beware of those you share it with as they may be an unwitting puppet for the spirits of darkness.

Made in the USA
Columbia, SC
18 February 2023

12641994R00050